What's the Angle?

Christopher Ryder

India | USA | UK

What's the Angle? © 2024 Christopher Ryder

All rights reserved.

No part of this publication may be reproduced, stored in a retrieval system, or transmitted, in any form or by any means, electronic, mechanical, photocopying, recording or otherwise, without the prior written permission of the presenters.

Christopher Ryder asserts the moral right to be identified as the author of this work.

Presentation by *BookLeaf Publishing*

Web: www.bookleafpub.com

E-mail: info@bookleafpub.com

ISBN: 9789360947309

First edition 2024

For HJR, my Son. Hopefully this is the first of many dedications.

ACKNOWLEDGEMENT

So many people have been instrumental to my growth and development as a writer. Namely, I would like to thank my wife Shannon for her undying support and encouragement in all of my creative pursuits. This book simply would not exist without her. Thank you also to Tommy Murphy: my creative mentor, my inspiration, my dearest brother in Christ. Many thanks to my own parents, Joseph and Dianne, as well as my mother-in-law and father-in-law, Rhonda Faye and Henry. To my brothers Aaron and Alex, my brother-in-law Brandon, thank you. Lastly, to my Pastors, Kurt and Horace, thank you for your prayers and guidance these many years. I have never lacked love and support. And for that, I thank my Lord and Savior Jesus Christ, above all else.

PREFACE

After years of false starts and plans that have gone awry, this will be my first completed volume of poetry. Huzzah! But there's only one problem ... what's the angle?

After all, I've tried my hand at a multitude of literary styles; and even now, having settled on poetry as my mode of personal expression, there remains a question of approach.

Is this a book of fanciful and embellished narratives making my life seem more exciting than it is? Is it a book of sappy lovesick limericks in which I will inevitably overshare and embarrass myself and my wife?

Perhaps instead I should choose not to shine a spotlight on myself, but as in all areas of my current life as a born-again Christian, endeavor to glorify God by means of honest, uplifting, meaningful poetry. That's it; that's the angle.

An Artist's Promise

I'd write for you, Wife,
But I don't know where to start
I'd draw for you, Wife,
But I've forgotten how to…art.

The stories are still there
Written somewhere
Hidden beneath my hair
Every pro and antagonist
They still exist
Yet my writer's block persists

I watch them all, Dear,
At the theater inside my head
I hear them all, Dear,
Like the music of the undead.

The films are numerous
Horrifying and humorous
Hindered by my hubris
And songs long for sound
Lyrics lie around
An artist's apathy abounds

I'll write it down, Love,
Even if I don't feel like it
Everything, my Love,
I promise to complete it.

When I Pray

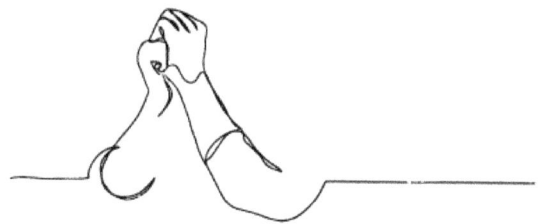

When I pray each day
I would like to say
That I talk to God
The very same way
That I talk to you…
But that's just not true

Because with you,
I have to hold back
I can only uplift
I shouldn't talk smack
Or gossip, complain,
My speech is restrained

But God doesn't judge
My emotional rants
God understands me
In a way you can't
He bears with my doubts
My God hears me out

It's insane to me
To think about it
The Creator hears
My inner bullshit
And doesn't smite me?
I think He likes me

When I pray each day
I thank God…a lot.
Because I'm humbled
By what I am not
He's holy, I sin
He lost so I'd win

Jesus died for me
I'm redeemed to God
I'm not a gambler
But I'll take those odds
Price paid for my crime
Deal of a lifetime

So pardon my prayer
The least I can do
Is to offer all
In praise to You
I'll pray, shout, and sing
I'll give everything

Because You did that…
Gave it all for me
I hope I'm worth it
Only One worthy
To Him be glory
For eternity

When I pray each day
I would like to say
That I talk to God
The very same way
That I talk to you…
But that's just not true

If you're curious
About this prayer stuff
Then give it a try
You can't get enough
Of the one who hears
And answers your prayers

Yearning for Snow

I may not have had a White Christmas
But I'm still yearning for snow
Oh, how I wish stormy stratus clouds
Could follow me wherever I go
I'd be a walking winter wonderland
A genuine Jack Frost
Calm and cool and collected
Snowballs ready to be tossed

An excuse to always bundle up tightly
In my finest Dickens attire
Or a big cozy cable-knit sweater
And hot cocoa by the fire
I'd press my face against the window
And watch the feathery flakes fall
All around, accumulating in pillowy piles
That are three, five, ten feet tall!

Cars and pavement begin to disappear
Beneath blankets of blustery bliss
Awaiting all the kids in the neighborhood
To play amidst the seasonal solstice
And though I'm too old for sledding
Or snow days off from school
I still relish flurries, snowfalls, and blizzards
Because snow is simply beautiful

I yearn for snow like I yearn for holiness
My darkness turning into light
The blood of Christ covering my misdeeds
My scarlet sins becoming white
So I'll keep watching the skies above
To see which way the weather will go
I'll be prepared for whatever comes
But I'm still yearning for snow

Overstimulated

My body sounded like a ramen packet this morning…
Creaking, cracking, crumbling,
Nothing like a reminder of old age to start the day.

My son joyfully jabbing my rib cage with his tiny feet…
Kicking, Squealing, Annoying,
My tyrannical toddler tormenter makes me say:

"You're just overstimulated,
Try to calm down,
You have to stay placated,
Don't have a breakdown."

So I put on his favorite YouTube songs to distract him…
Singing, Clapping, Droning,
And I try to zone out on my phone to distract myself.

But before I know it, he starts hiccuping over and over…
Hiccuping, Hiccuping, Hiccuping,
And going downstairs to get him a drink, I say to myself:

"You're just overstimulated,
Try to calm down,
You have to stay placated,
Don't have a breakdown."

So breakfast time comes and I strap him to his high chair…
Eating, Munching, Drooling,
Then I turn on the TV; a most reliable babysitter.

I barely have enough time to finish a bowl of cereal before…
Crying, Fussing, Whining,
I return to find he's flung food on the floor, so I whisper:

"You're just overstimulated,
Try to calm down,
You have to stay placated,
Don't have a breakdown."

Better get out of the house, so I thought we'd try a movie…
Entertaining, Engaging, Distracting,
He fell asleep, I was at peace, at least for a little bit.
His nap cut short, and on the drive home, he didn't go back to sleep…
Crying, Fussing, Whining,
I accelerated and my drink fell over, and I shouted, "DAMMIT!"

I was just overstimulated,
I couldn't calm down,
It can't be understated;
I had a breakdown.

So I cleaned up the sticky cherry soda, every little bit…
Cleaning, Scrubbing, Wiping,
As my son was still squirming in his seat behind me.

We got home, went upstairs, and into bed, both of us…
Laying, Resting, Drifting,
And off to sleep he went again, and I felt guilty.

He was just overstimulated
From all the screen time,
I made him overstimulated
Just to have some "Me Time".

If you're feeling overstimulated
You might need to walk away,
But peace can't be simulated…
Sometimes, you just need to pray.

My Golden Hour

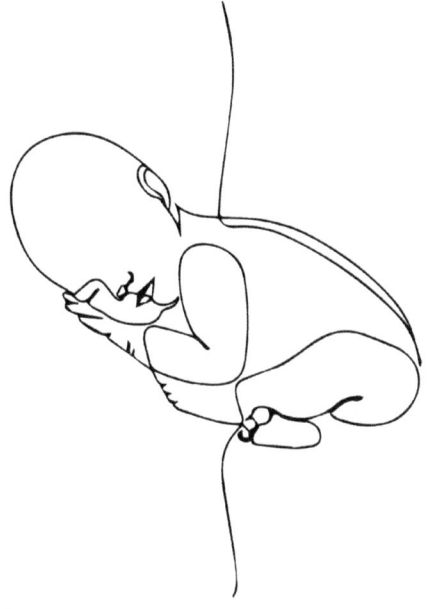

Morning time is such a treasure
I guess that's why they call it the "Golden Hour"
But never do I find more pleasure
Than in watching my son's sweet slumber

How I marvel at his skin
A canvas on which only God's paintbrush imbues
As the sunlight trickles in
And kisses his chubby cheeks with warm hues

His stillness is sometimes concerning
Like a doll, he lies there, unbothered and frozen
And yet, I find it still so comforting
When his face twitches to life with subtle motion

I can only watch with expectant joy
As his nose crinkles, his eyes wince, and his mouth whimpers,
But then I lay my hand on my little boy,
"It's okay Baby, Daddy's here," is my simple whisper

And off he goes, back to sleep
To dream of things and places I can't even imagine
But this time is mine to keep
My Golden Hour, my treasure, my slumbering Son.

Nostalg-ick

Facebook shows me memories on the daily
So that I'm not living day-to-day,
But yesterday-to-yesterday,
And it's not okay…

These memories are cringeworthy at best
And traumatizing at worst,
A toxic timeline that's cursed,
And yet, I still thirst…

Yes, like a masochistic melancholy montage,
The photos and status updates play,
The tragic hero I used to portray,
The words I would say…

An increasingly younger version of myself
Moans and drones about "love",
A concept he knows nothing of,
Not looking above…

He was aimless and faithless and selfish
And I wish he would just die.
But he did…didn't I?
Didn't I too die?

These are just memories, like a dog's vomit,
I wasn't meant to ever return,
I was just supposed to learn,
Leave the chaff to burn.

Christ made me a new man; a new creation!
And I was raised from the dead,
And every word I ever said
Henceforth: Deleted.

A Hater Loved

Oh, what a double-minded son I've been to a
Father I supposedly adore,
How often have I been praising and all of the
sudden ignore,
How many times would I be praying and
accidentally snore,
Because I've fallen asleep, because sometimes
God is just a bore.

Oh, what a fickle friend I've been to the King whom I serve,
How often have I driven down His path and suddenly swerve,
How many traffic signs did I fail to observe,
Because I was too focused on things I didn't deserve.

Oh, what a faithless follower I've been to my teacher and Savior,
How often have I portrayed unbelief in my careless behavior,
How many times must I learn that God is not a performance-grader,
Because if He was, then I'd always be marked as a failure.

Oh, what a predictability I've become in the eyes of the Accuser,
How often have I written under the pen name, "Self-Abuser",
How many times have I looked in the mirror and only saw a loser,
Because if self-hatred is a drug, I guess you'd call me a user.

Oh, what a spectacle I've made of my sinful condition,
How often do I write songs of praise rather than dirges of conviction,
How many more words will be wasted on dishonorable diction,
Because I'm tired of writing and whining when I'm a new creation.

Oh, what a great and good Father have we received
How often has He spoken the truth when we've been deceived
How many wounds and sorrows has He healed and relieved
Because He really does love us, more than we can possibly perceive.

Oh yes, what a glorious gift have we freely received!
How often has He blessed us from the time we first believed
How many moments has He called us to come and cleave,
Because it is His love that says, "I will never leave."

My Town

I'm no historian or scholar,
But I know Dale City like the back of my hand!

That's…probably not true either.
I'm rubbish with directions, but understand
That after 30 years in this town,
I have some stories to write down.

Now, I'm pretty white bread and milquetoast,
So my tales aren't that tall or fanciful.
Don't have much for which to boast
For a town that's just adjacent to our nation's capital;
A place Dale's citizens rarely visit,
But most do commute to it.

But for the rest of us regular shlubs,
We're resigned to retail or fast food service,
Either selling bathtubs or footlong subs;
Living paycheck to paycheck makes one nervous.
Not that I have much to complain about,
I live in the suburbs, how's that for clout?

My town is always and forever changing,
That CVS used to be a Roy Rogers, y'know…
And we're always and forever complaining
About which crappy casual dining place to go.
I always preferred Red Robin for endless fries,
Even though the burgers are better at Five Guys.

We used to have things to brag about though,
Potomac Mills: Record-Holder for Largest Outlet Mall!
But then they replaced Vans skatepark with a Costco…
Not sure if that was an upgrade or pitfall.
I rarely patronize the place anymore…
Save for the odd visit to the Lego Store.

And yet, some places are institutions,
Like the AMC Theater, which I still frequent.
For moviegoing, there's no substitution,
Except the Alamo Drafthouse when it's convenient.
Speaking of movie houses, there's one more to mention;
A place that deserves special attention.

When I was growing up in Dale City,
There was a Dollar Theater a stone's throw away.
Where in my youth, I watched many a movie,
But it's not a movie theater today…
It's now a humble little local fellowship;
A church at which I serve and worship.

My favorite place when I was a child
Is now my workplace and occupation.
And I think the circumstances were wild,
But I met my destiny at this destination.
Not 8 years ago, on a bright Sunday morn, Did
my future wife walk through that door.

Turns out, she'd grown up here as well,
Though our paths had somehow never crossed.
It's funny how a place you know so well
Can help you find something you'd thought lost:
Love…for stories, for journeys, for ups and
downs,
For the brick and mortar that is my hometown.

An Ode to the River Shannon

I asked God for a bride
And He gave me a river
And I am satisfied
Supplied with her water

Quenched by her kindness
Drenched in her affection
Salve for my blindness
Clarity for my reflection

I am steeped in stability
Sopping wet in support
Waist deep in security
Anchored in her port

I drink in her beauty
I bathe in her grace
Like dark brewed tea
The color of her face

Drown me in your love
Submerge me in ecstasy
Baptize me in the Name of
All that is holy and lovely

I'll swim the longest channels
I'll brave the deepest depths
Any expedition, I will travel
And I will give my last breath

My sister, my cistern
Be filled to overflowing
May your waters churn
For the winds are blowing

And the waves climb higher
Obstructing the light of day
We will stick together
Even if we get washed away

Life sprang from her spring
Like Moses from the Nile
So came our first offspring
So strong, and yet, so fragile

The river birthed a miracle
Made of blood, sweat, and tears
Reducing her to a puddle
But extinguishing our fears

We asked God for a family
And He gave us an ocean
Deeper than the Irish Sea
Longer than the River Shannon

So our love will still grow
In every measurable way
The water will still flow
As long as there is night and day

Employee of the Month

I will not exalt myself
I will not ascend
Up a corporate ladder
With rungs made of faces
That I should tread upon them
With disregard
Disrespect
Disenchanted
Disenfranchised
They would praise me though
Because they know
I'm just on my grind
And grapes must be squashed
To make my wine
Yes, I shall drink
And I shall eat and be merry

A short break
On my way
To the cherry on top
I've earned my rest
I've stood the test
I deserve an escalator
An elevator
An exalt-ator
Take me there!
Where's my chariot?
Where's the fanfare?
I demand to speak to the manager!

Pride cometh before the fall
And I've got the bruises to prove it
I show them off
As if I didn't deserve it
I asked for this!
I'm a masochist!
And it all stems from selfish ambition
A tree that's never satisfied
No matter how tall it grows
I should be going low
I should be washing feet
Be more selfless
Show more kindness
Ask for forgiveness
And maybe sin less

I will not exalt myself
I will not take the hill
Humility will be my ministry
And charity my salary
I will race to the bottom
To be last in line
To become a servant of all
A new wineskin for new wine
And no matter how many slices
Of humble pie I have to eat
My true food will always be
To do the will of the One
Who sent me

Midpoint

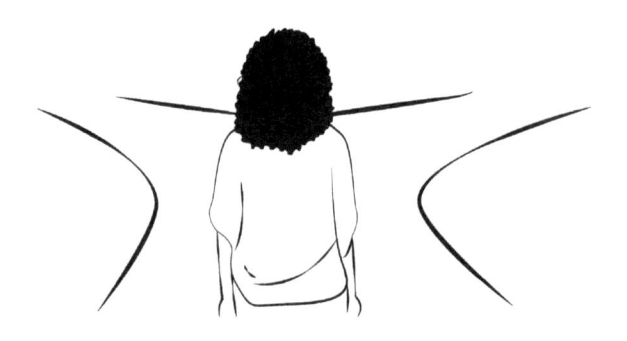

And so here I am;
At a crossroads?
Well, who knows?
I could just sit and wait for a sign
A billboard would serve me just fine
Because I'm not goin' till God goes ahead
If I lived like that, I'd probably be dead
Sometimes God doesn't want to be your compass
But He does want to be your conscience
What I mean is, "Walk by faith, not by sight,"
Because our God is simply not a streetlight
We say, "Jesus, take the wheel,"
As if He didn't give us the automobile
Don't you have a license?
Am I making sense?

He wants to guide you, not control you!
He wants to provide for you, not patrol you!
We are His treasured possession
Not an empty vessel for possession
A relationship can't be one-sided
Just like one flesh can't be divided
We are married to the Lord our God
I know that sounds incredibly odd

But as such, we yield our individuality
In favor of spiritual unity
And sometimes, He makes His plans clear
And sometimes, the roadmap disappears
But if you can't see the next step on your journey
Do you think He'd let you stumble if you walk humbly?
It's about trust
So quit sitting in the dust
Get on your feet, and keep on going!
Come on, your lack of faith is showing!
Don't miss out on what comes next
Just because you're waiting for God to text
He's already given us more than we need
Just a mustard seed is enough to proceed
Don't worry about what's behind you
Past pillars of salt will only blind you
There's more to your story, just turn the page
Intermission is over, time to set the stage

This isn't your last life lost
Nor is it the final boss
It's just a checkpoint…
Every book needs a midpoint
And so here I am;
At a crossroads?
Well, who knows?
I could go this way or that way
As long as I know the Way

Nocturnal Tears

I've been crying in my sleep
Maybe that's the only time I can
Closed like a tin my emotions I keep
Trying to repress for the sake of man
Hood covering a tear-stained face
Away from day-dwellers, stay woke
Up in the light, seems far away like space
Out there, but in here, so close I could choke
Because Your Word tastes bitter now
Now that's not fair, I'm just lashing out

Here I stand, punching at the Wind somehow
Out of breath again, yet my thoughts still shout
Violent, yet silent, compliant
To my dreamscape, come what may
I remind myself that I am reliant
On or off, the Light within will stay
Lit is the fire of one who is desperate
Yet I am too afraid to speak a peep
This man will not allow his cheeks to get wet
With sadness I weep, but only in my sleep.

Woke

I woke up this morning with a headache,
backache, and an earache,
Because instead of the word of God, I listened to satan's mixtape
Y'know, he has no shortage of lies to try and bully, brand, and break
And I give audience to him, even though I know his power is fake
"Know thy self, know thy enemy,"
I guess that was my first mistake

I'll go back to sleep, try again tomorrow, hoping for one thing when I wake:
Your new mercies

I woke up this morning with a hangover and a mind full of regret
See, I'm always looking at my past, even though they say, "Don't do it!"
But those who don't study history are only doomed to repeat it
And this dog is about sick of returning again to his own vomit
I lost the taste for it years ago, so I guess that makes me an addict?
I'll try to sleep it off for now, get some rest, and pray for respite;
Your new mercies

I woke up this morning breathing, alive and new, all because of You
I didn't complain or feel depressed, I simply delighted in light of You
I wasn't burdened, anxious, or ashamed, but I still needed to
Lean on You, trust in You, love You in everything I think, say, and do
Because I'm still as weak as I was yesterday, this much I know is true

But You woke me up today, and that is enough
reason to praise You
For Your new mercies

Jiminy Jonah's Jeering

A stream of consciousness
Flows like screams from my conscience
And Jiminy Cricket was dressed so well, but he
Was still swallowed, swaddled in the belly of a whale
Oh, the questions I'd ask of Jonah
The first man with claustrophobia
What darkness must he have seen
In miles and miles of small intestine
Oh, the grossness of it all, to be spat up like gall
I wonder if he was lukewarm or just indigestible
O, Monstro! Meistro of the Maelstrom!
At least you could've chewed me up like common bubblegum
But now, at the sea shore, I'm unsure

The people before me are premature
Unprepared for required repentance
How can I utter a single sentence?
Never mind Nineveh, our nation needs no novice
A man with conviction, diction, prediction of a promise
And if he's successful, then he's more super than Superman
Hero to the helpless, and harbinger of God's grand plan
But that prophet is not me, not yet
And due to my self-doubt, I bet
Just consider me still in gestation
Indigestion with no expectation
Don't call on me to go make disciples
I lack discipline; it's a vicious cycle.

A Snow Day for MLK

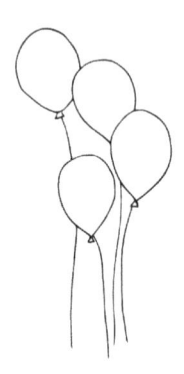

The first snowfall of the year came to Dale City
On January 15th, 2024; a Monday
But not some mundane Monday, but Martin
Luther King Jr. Day
And as daylight crested and snowflakes rested
upon the ground,
I couldn't help but be struck with a sense of
cruel irony

For to watch the rugged and trod upon black pavement
Be covered by invasive, cold, indifferent white snow
Seemed to be the most gentle gentrification I'd ever seen
But perhaps I was overthinking it, as always
After all, I had been yearning for snow;
Sweet, sublime, substantial snow
Why shouldn't it fall on Dr. King's Birthday?
I'm sure he wouldn't mind…or maybe it would be the last thing on his mind
But never mind, shouldn't I be excited about this? It's what I've been waiting for
But the cold was numbing my fingers,
Which I needed to scoop up the fresh dog poop from the grass
What a way to celebrate the late great freedom fighter…
And later, after reuniting with my mixed-race son,
I decided to snap a few photos in the snow, just for fun
Now there's a testament to MLK's dream; a half-white/half-black toddler
Being posed by his dear old dad for an inevitable Instagram post
What chills me most is that I almost included a hashtag for #MLKday

My wife was mad I didn't put a coat on him
But the coat would've ruined the aesthetic
Now, a word of advice to my readership:
Prioritizing aesthetic over your son's health and your wife's peace is pretty pathetic
But at least the pics came out good, so…worth it?
I don't know if MLK wanted it this way, if he even wanted a holiday
But I just wanted my perfect snow day
And not have to think about his words or his legacy
But it's not about me or my nostalgic comforts
It's about remembrance, it's about reverence, it's about repentance
I took time tonight to seek out some insight
Into the man himself, Dr. Martin Luther King Jr.
And this is what he had to say:
"The shape of the world today
Does not permit us the luxury of soft-mindedness.
A nation or a civilization that continues to produce soft-minded men
Purchases its own spiritual death
on an installment plan."
"Soft-minded" describes me all too shamefully
I mean, are you kidding me? It's enough to make my heart break.
I am but a frigid and fragile little snowflake.

But pity parties will have to wait; that's not the way to celebrate
And it's not too late to make a change, however small
After all, the snowfall seems to have given us a clean slate
Another quote to end this ramble; not from MLK, but from the Bible
In Isaiah 1:18, the saying goes:
"Come now, let us reason together, says the LORD:
Though your sins are like scarlet,
they shall be as white as snow."

Project

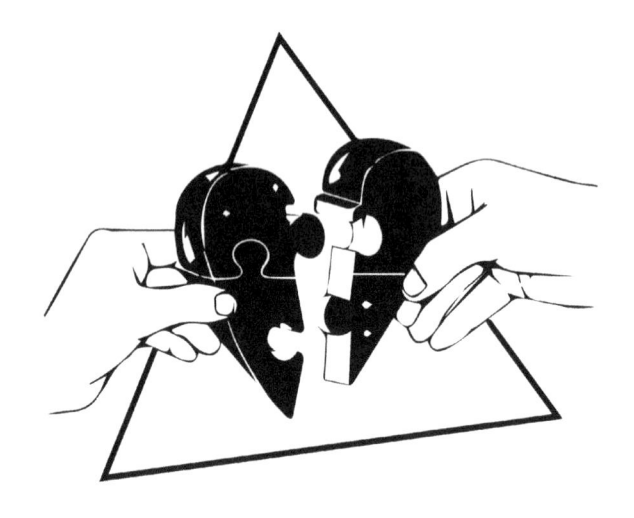

I think I've discovered recently
(Well, God has revealed it to me, really)
That there's an involuntary calamity
That can strike a relationship cruelly
It's when every aspect of genuine love
Becomes idolatry
You know, "idolatry"? That word that tastes like poison
And we can't bear to imagine that maybe…just MAYBE
Our "best intentions" have become a fallacy!

It's like this fantasy that we have to protect,
Interject, and perfect the very…object
Of our affection, unaffectionately
Known as…our project

You know God made us to love each other?
He fashioned us for compassion, passionately
Produced us perfectly in the image of Christ
We think we're just being nice
When we reach out, like it's our "Christian duty"
But empathy isn't just a good quality
It's a gift we receive when the Spirit dwells in us bodily
Follow me, because I need to be clear
Love is the most important thing in all existence
If it is sincere

So when you see someone who's broken and lost,
Do you stop to listen to their plight?
Or do you give them a 10-step program
That will "lead them to the light"?
After all, "God can only help those who help themselves,"
Right?
But if that's true, then His grace is void
And if there's no grace, then we have been employed
As messengers of His word under false pretense

It's like saying the shed blood of Christ was pointless

I mean, are we out to speak the truth in love to our lost brethren?
Or are we DIY Christians making projects "suitable" for Heaven?
And oh, what a thing of beauty
Are our finished products to behold!
How proud we are to make
Such wretches reformed and brought into the fold

Truth be told,
I think we might as well be making calves of gold because the idol you've made of them
Is an idol in the image of you alone
We have exchanged the glory of the eternal God
For idols of flesh and bone
And we know how we compare our "righteousness"
With theirs' and we give our charitable wares
Casting pearls before swine in our minds, unfair
I mean, do we actually care?

Could we be like Jesus with the adulteress
And say, "Nor do I condemn you"?

Or would we cast the stones of our own accusation
To the degradation of someone "beneath" you?
And I know I'm speaking things that offend the mind
Because none of us want to believe we're actually blind
Blinded not by rebellion, but selfishness
Too proud to recognize our defiance
Of Christ-likeness
Or is it really just me who's forsaken self-sacrifice?

But forgive me, for I've misled you
This rhetoric is not to rebuke you
Or even to teach you a lesson
This is just my confession
I know I need a selfless love
A gift from above that forgives my hypocrisy
I want to stop living in false humility
I want to love extravagantly
Cleansed from ALL iniquity
Oh Father, won't You please forgive me?
I need You Jesus to renew my identity!

Aren't you grateful, aren't you glad
That we aren't just imperfect projects
To our Holy and ever-loving Dad?
That He actually loves us perfectly

Completely and unconditionally?
See, sometimes my poetry
Is just a cleverly-written apology
Written and spoken to everyone EXCEPT
The intended recipient
See, I need to repent
And here's where it gets personal
However informal, here's my repentance
Because sometimes it's easier to do a performance
Than to admit my regret
But still, I'm sorry that I've treated you like just another project

Breathing Machine

I've been breathing for 34 years, hardly "young"
But most of that was a hacking cough
With a dehydrated tongue, and an iron lung
Luckily, no one turned my life support off

I am nothing but a breathing machine
But my hardware was hard-wired
For the most obscene sins ever seen
As seen on TV, televised hellfire

We're all just secular screen-slavers
World Wide Web wastoids
Prone to sinfully salacious behaviors
Use our phones like opioids

Anything to distract us from reality
Medicinal memes like laughing gas
Breathing fumes of moronic immorality
Groupthink assumptions stink like ass

I am but a hopeless breathing machine
And I could use a factory reset
I have viruses that need to be cleaned
And an internet history full of regret

But every machine has its Maker
Every CPU with built-in IOU
Mine put in a fresh circuit breaker
And now I'm running like new!

I am a living, breathing, human being
With a new operating system
I no longer run on whims or feelings
But I am controlled by wisdom

My mistake was thinking my breath was mine
That I could possibly trace its origins
But your breath and mine are both divine
We were just dust; dismal dirt-denizens

But no longer should we walk this way
Conforming to the world's patterns
Let's commit instead to a higher Way
The path of righteousness matters

We're not robots or mechanical suits
Just waiting for a capable pilot
We're more like trees bearing fruits
In search of a temperate climate

I've been breathing for 34 years, hardly old
But now, my breath is unobstructed
I still get the odd flu or COVID or head cold
But my inner workings have been reconstructed

Mystery and Adventure

Something is calling out to me
Outside of my comfort zone
But its author is a mystery
And its whereabouts, unknown

It's a quiet, compelling voice
Beckoning me outdoors
Yet it still gives me the choice
To venture past familiar shores

Beyond my residential walls
Far from the day-to-day
Someone continuously calls
Wanting to whisk me away

"To where?" I wistfully wonder
Though scared to hear an answer
"Anywhere and everywhere!"
It echoes somewhere in the ether

"To playgrounds and hometowns
Swimming in creeks for fun
Showing no fear of sundowns
But always ready to run…"

"To train tracks and bushwhacks
And 7-11 after dark
From Woodbridge to Fairfax
And treks through Eakin Park…"

"To late nights and play fights
And all of it caught on video
Sleepovers with no nightlights
Is a dreamlike scenario…"

"To demos and house shows
Music like you've never heard
Like clothes from Yesterday's Rose
Equally artistic and absurd…"

"To basements and pavements
To play dodgeball or spoons
There are simply no replacements
For those sunny Sunday afternoons…"

"I'll take you on an adventure,"
The voice promises to me
"It'll be like a thirst-quencher,
To satisfy your latent memory…"

I haven't yet taken a sip
But Adventure is still calling
I so long to retake that trip
So why am I still stalling?
Perhaps I'll put it all on hold
And tend to my life as it is now
But if it comes knocking, I'm told,
His invite will be hard to disavow

So I'll keep a bag packed to go
And a camcorder close at hand
Because you just never know
What Adventure has planned.

Bubbles

I blow bubbles with my son
My son who's almost two
It's simple, but so much fun
It's our favorite thing to do

Bubbles, like Bubble Guppies,
His newest TV obsession
Together, we pretend to be fishies
Swimming in the endless ocean

Bubbles, like at Disney World,
We wanted to buy you a bubble wand
But just like every little boy and girl
The bubbles were all you could want

Bubbles, like bubble baths,
Where hygiene and playtime meet
Oh how I love your little laugh
When I wash your tiny feet

Bubbles, like your popper toy,
How it keeps you distracted
But, I want to blow bubbles with my boy
Have you forgotten your Dad?

You blow bubbles with me!
See? Isn't this so much fun?
Oh, but now you're flying freely
When did you learn to run?

I blow bubbles with my son
My son who's almost two
But when the bubbles are all gone
What am I going to do?

Bubbles, like in Mommy's belly,
When we first saw your ultrasound
The probe sliding across cold jelly
Your fetal form floating around

Bubbles, like in the NICU,
The Isolette where you slept
I'd open the door to touch you
But for 7 weeks, we wept

Bubbles, so fragile are they,
Here in an instant, gone in a pop,
Like memories, they drift away
I wish I could rewind, pause, or stop

How much longer will he be playful?
The second year has gone like the first
How much longer will he giggle?
How long until the bubble bursts?
I'll keep blowing bubbles with him
So long as I have air in my lungs
And I'll tell him I'll always love him
Even when he's no longer young

Come Back

I can't make you believe again
I can't lighten the load in your pack
I can't stand to see you leave again
So I'm asking you, please come back

I can't reconstruct your faith
I can't give you all the answers you lack
I can't go on and on with this debate
But I'm asking you, please come back

I can't undo the abuse you endured
I can't back your retaliatory attack
I can't help that you've been injured
But I'm asking you, please come back

I can't loosen the ties that bind
I can't unchain you from the rack
I can't open the doors of your mind
But I'm asking you, please come back

I can't find out what went wrong
I can't help if you refuse to crack
I can't keep pretending to be strong
So I'm asking you, please come back

I can't fix the damage done
I can't pick up someone else's slack
I can't promise it'll be fun
But I'm asking you, please come back

I can't make the decision for you
I can't blaze the trail that you'll track
I can't convince you that I love you
But I'm asking you, please come back

I can't take back what's been spoken
I can't travel back to when we first began
I can't heal what's been broken
I can't…but Jesus Christ can

So come back to Him, my brother
I can promise you He's all you need
So come back to Him, my sister
Whom the Son sets free is free indeed

What's the Angle?

I'll write a book of poetry
You'll ask, "What's the angle?"
I'll say, "This isn't geometry,"
"And there is no angle."

But if there was one to record
I think it would have to be right
It's the one that looks up and forward
Sorry to be so black and white

Because I know what it's like
To go the wrong direction
To swing and miss every strike
Always falling short of perfection

The right way is not my way
The right angle is straight and narrow
The right way is not mine to say
But it is my duty to share, so…

Jesus is the only Way,
Truth, and Life forevermore
The reality is night and day
Of this I'm never more sure

So yes, there is an angle
Congrats, you cracked the code
But there was no mystery to untangle
I just gave you the answer I owed

And now you've heard my answer
Now I've got just one question:
"How does your life measure
When compared to perfection?"

Printed in the USA
CPSIA information can be obtained
at www.ICGtesting.com
LVHW021352050724
784681LV00005B/1157